The Sacraments

of Desire

_____

1 9 9 1

Other books

by Linda Gregg

Too Bright to See

Alma

T h e

Sacraments
of Desire

Linda Gregg

Graywolf Press

Some of the poems in this book first appeared in the following magazines: *American Poetry Review, Antaeus, The Atlantic, Black Warrior Review, Indiana Review, Ironwood, Massachusetts Review, New Letters, The Paris Review, Partisan Review, Pequod, Ploughshares, Poetry East, The Quarterly, Sonora Review,* and *The Taos Review.*

Publication of this volume is made possible in part by grants from the National Endowment for the Arts and the Minnesota State Arts Board, with funds provided through an appropriation by the Minnesota State Legislature. Graywolf Press is the recipient of a McKnight Foundation Award administered by the Minnesota State Arts Board and receives generous contributions from corporations, foundations, and individuals. Graywolf Press is a member agency of United Arts, Saint Paul.

Published by Graywolf Press
250 Third Avenue North
Suite 600
Minneapolis, Minnesota 55401

Library of Congress Cataloging-in-Publication Data

Gregg, Linda.
The sacraments of desire / Linda Gregg.
p.   cm.
ISBN 978-1-55597-173-1
I. Title
PS3557.R433S24 1991
811'.54—dc20   90-21206

For my mother

FRANCES RUNDALL GREGG

I want Her always standing as beautiful as the power

that makes lambs and birds.

The Sacraments of Desire

PART ONE

Part One

Glistening

As I pull the bucket from the crude well,
the water changes from dark to a light
more silver than the sun. When I pour it
over my body that is standing in the dust
by the oleander bush, it sparkles easily
in the sunlight with an earnestness like
the spirit close up. The water magnifies
the sun all along the length of it.
Love is not less because of the spirit.
Delight does not make the heart childish.
We thought the blood thinned, our weight
lessened, that our substance was reduced
by simple happiness. The oleander is thick
with leaves and flowers because of spilled
water. Let the spirit marry the heart.
When I return naked to the stone porch,
there is no one to see me glistening.
But I look at the almond tree with its husks
cracking open in the heat. I look down
the whole mountain to the sea. Goats bleating
faintly and sometimes bells. I stand there
a long time with the sun and the quiet,
the earth moving slowly as I dry in the light.

Ordinary Songs

Dull with pneumonia, wrapped on the porch,
I watch the wind darken parts of the smooth sea
again and again. Watch the sheen return
each time a lighter color. The Greek woman
sings as if the sky were listening.
Ordinary songs. About a man gone long enough
for her to know he's gone always. Songs like that.
Sings easily and loud over the quiet water
to where the sky disappears. Sheep eating
and bells ringing. I think of the roofs
in Massachusetts with the gray sky above
and the blind man walking in the snow as the train
shook everything passing near us. I think of us
all wanting the gods to touch our skin. Our hearts
blessing the slender bare trees in American lots
of bearded dry weeds. I have come here
for the trial by grace, by loneliness. Remembering
the girl I started as trying to know the earth
with her body, the touch of the bark all she had.
Trying to find her way to the love women know.
I have brought myself to these hot fields of dark
red poppies and the quiet cove over there.
Shepherds and fishermen and the happy women
in black who give me milk and fish while everything
blooms and I accept gratefully. Listening to doves,

I grow sleepy and dream of a still world where space
looks like the sound owls make at night. A world
without color that knows the sea's dark blue.
Without people, but knows the dancer and marble form.
Without light, but knows the fire it came from.
I sleep as a shard weary from earthquakes moving earth
an inch at a time, tilting each thing. The sea
wearing away the land. Everything stronger than me.
On the shard a reclining naked woman kissed by a god.

Surrounded by Sheep and Low Ground

When death comes, we take off our clothes
and gather everything we left behind:
what is dark, broken, touched with shame.
When Death demands we give an accounting,
naked we present our lives in bundles.
See how much these weigh, we tell him,
refusing to deny what we have lived.
Everything that is touched by light
loves the light. We the stubborn-as-grass,
we who reel at the taste of sap and want
our spirits cleansed, will not betray
the weeds, snake, or crippled mare.
Never leave behind what the light shone on.

On Lesbos Remembering Her Mountain on Paros

I am back in Greece after three years
of watching my face grow older in the mirror.
I look for Her in a bean field near this crude house,
watch for Her on sides of hills facing the sea.
She is not at the sites. Not the one with collapsed
marble by a tree, nor the one where there is
nothing left but flowers. I do not want to let go.
Like a child wanting the mother's hand,
I do not want Her undone as time undoes.
As nature and wind and finally sun undo.
I want Her always standing as beautiful as the power
that makes lambs and birds. I do not want a lady
fading and leaving me alone with the hard earth.
I have kept mock-orange and white roses in a vase
three days in my room as I read and write and try
to dream Her back again. They shrivel and the roses
are suddenly heavier than the stems can hold up.
They smell as good, but are a shame. My failing
without Her. I am left with roses sinking in heat
and not anyone even walking away, or disappearing,
refusing to be seen. Not even someone being lost.

The Small Thing Love Is

My body is filled by a summer of lust
and I can't tell the difference between desire,
longing, and all the sweet speeches
love hoards. Something deeper grinds its teeth
on metal, mocks and preens in cold rooms
where a glass breaks and women wear
rich gowns that weigh more than they do.
Death mating with Beauty. Night roaring
and the cathedral holding its ground
against the strength and purring
of the wet couple undone
by a power only the earth could love.

Ahdaam Kai Ava

I came the whole way around from going out
to cliffs and oceans and edges
where I stood with all my strength
begging and singing and weeping, and came back
to this makeshift farmyard where my little ones
sleep in the toilet at night with the door
held closed with a rock. They dance
with webbed feet all day in the water.
They begin to sing as soon as I let them
out into the morning; and no matter what
I am or how I feel, my heart no bigger
than theirs refuses to keep still and I
listen intently. Harmonize in the silence
of myself with their unimportance:
their elegant, unimportant happiness.

All the Spring Lends Itself to Her

If Her skirt does not bend the grass, nor sea air
mold Her shape while She is happy, there is no grace.
I will not stop looking for that. Song and color
circle in this air for Her to stand in.
If She does not come to take pleasure in this giving,
all things will reverse to alms and penitence.
She is not needed for this world to be a success.
Either way the other powers will have their time.
But if spring comes and She is absent, we will eat
food without sacrament, our hearts not renewed
for the other seasons: the one where we give, the one
where we are taken, and the season where we are lost
in the darkness. If love does not reign,
we are unsuited for the season of ripeness.
If we do not see Her body in the glass of this beauty,
the sun will blind us. We will lie in the humming fields
and call to Her, coaxing Her back. We will lie
pressed close to the earth, calling Her name,
wondering if it is Her voice we are whispering.

Greece When Nobody's Looking

The earth bleached pale by two thousand years.
Poppies and weeds blooming in the tough fields.
Stillness and olive trees.
I asked a young woman if she made things,
woven or sewed. No, she said, we don't care.
The sea is calm today as ever it was in May.
And the moon almost full. A poetry
of stars and stone and the ordinary.

The Letter

I am not feeling strong yet, but I am taking
good care of myself. The weather is perfect.
I read and walk all day and then walk to the sea.
I expect to swim soon. For now I am content.
I am not sure what I hope for. I feel I am
doing my best. It reminds me of when I was
sixteen dreaming of Lorca, the gentle trees outside
and the creek. Perhaps poetry replaces something
in me that others receive more naturally.
Perhaps my happiness proves a weakness in my life.
Even my failures in poetry please me.
Time is very different here. It is very good
to be away from public ambition.
I sweep and wash, cook and shop.
Sometimes I go into town in the evening
and have pastry with custard. Sometimes I sit
at a table by the harbor and drink half a beer.

Night Music

She sits on the mountain that is her home
and the landscapes slide away. One goes down
and then up to the monastery. One drops away
to a winnowing ring and a farmhouse where a girl
and her mother are hanging the laundry.
There's a tiny port in the distance where
the shore reaches the water. She is numb
and clear because of the grieving in that world.
She thinks of the bandits and soldiers who
return to the places they have destroyed.
Who plant trees and build walls and play music
in the village square evening after evening,
believing the mothers of the boys they killed
and the women they raped will eventually come
out of the white houses in their black dresses
to sit with their children and the old.
Will listen to the music with unreadable eyes.

My Father and God

The rain comes down on the desert and the next day,
my father knew, the earth is covered with tiny flowers.
He abandoned us every year, four daughters and a wife.
Drove with gallons of water tied along both sides
of the jeep to lie on his stomach at sunrise on sand
and stone surrounded by rock and sand. To know distance
and know the close-up. Because he believed it was near
to God. The place nobody wanted. The parts of the world
left alone. The flatness where things are broken down
to the clearest form. He would say it was the simple
he wanted. Sun coming up and shining first on the bottom
of your feet as you are looking at flowers appearing
out of sand. A lizard lying on a hot stone knowing
the lightning wants to strike something. Knowing lightning
has no mouth, no teeth, not even a stomach; but when
it strikes, the lizard will race wriggling up to God's
shining face, which is so bright that no one can see
anything but the glare. The sun is always there or dark.
Far off or close up. My father lived out where God could
kill him. That is the way of real desire. The way of
passionate grace, slow or quick, the small and the big.
Absolute as two hands rubbing together with sand on them,
the grit between. It is what makes the heart seem tender.
Only this. But my father died in the grand house he built
with his own hands on the snow line next to an Indian midden.

(Not on top, he said, because he wanted the quail families to continue their walks together like that always.) My sister thought he was playing when he fell down next to the half-finished chess game by the fire that night, making a huge animal sound. It was just like a bear roaring, she said.

Tokens of What She Is

The golden lady seven feet tall dies in the mind.
I hear bells and then make out the silvery-gray
backs of sheep grazing in the moonlight.
Stone under feet and beauty under tall pines.
All of it held sadly in my heart with awe.
Neither day nor night can I find Her.
What I find in pieces on plowed land and sea wall
of hand, breast and skirt does not come alive again.
Comes not out of the distance, is only the product
of my longing. A breeze billows the doorway
curtain into the dark lower room of my house.
I continue on female with the small wind
in the almond leaves. Some would call it tenderness,
but part of me calls it pale. Wants the trees to be
leg-warmers to Her giant standing. Joy reigning.
She giving, knowing we are tokens of what She is.
What comes to flower and bears. Lovers, poets, fools
like singers for that world which will not come to me.
The lack which I am. Which gives me speech.
My voice as clues to Her absent grace.

The Design inside Them

At six every night the women sit on chairs
under vine leaves or out on the street in front
of the houses on whitewashed rocks crocheting.
The talk in Greek is too fast for me, but I can tell
it is about prices in Mytilene compared to here.
They make pictures of flowers and leaves and birds
with white string to cover the windows,
tables and pillows. One of the women serves me
a piece of cake in syrup and a glass of water.
A daughter comes through the billowing curtain
in the doorway. She is fifteen and wants a Walkman
and goes away. She will never be like them.
Her little sister goes from the mother and stands
near a man who is feeding olive branches to his goat.
Then to the new kittens and back to her mother.
Sits quiet in the chatter and industry, and then away
again to the kittens and the man. As though
a string is tied to her waist and unravels like
their idea of justice and good and gentle kindness.
Gathers up again as the old swallows and flowers.

Of Absence

I climb the mountain.
Up steps the moon has already taken.
Of absence. Of things broken.
To see if the moon is a mouth.
To see if I am what it wants.

Coleridge Saw the Harp as
Invented Beyond Nature's Reason

Is it true women are the most supple form
of agreement with the real?
Do they make harps of themselves,
singing with their earned bodies?
Machines of sentiment the universe
blows through, that winter comes to
as it does to stone? These song-for-song,
self-for-love, beaten as all exiles are.
These that the Earth quickly cares nothing for.

How You Can Know Her

Neither with nor without a lover.
Neither singing nor silent. She is either
putting on or taking off her clothes.
The water is for bathing, for washing the porch.
The house is either hers or she is a stranger
standing hidden in the trees about to be called.
She will walk easily to the door or run away.
She is either clothed in night or naked
in white silk. If she has jewelry, it was given.
If not, she doesn't mind.
She carries a love in her as a rose has its scent.

To Be Like That

Anything to move ahead, to get there.
Wanting to be licked clean by the rough tongue
of what She is. Searching for it.
Leaving cow, carcass and blood to enter silence,
to go to the island and stand among olive trees
looking down on cove after cove of blue water,
on the Earth where a man brings his sheep
in the morning and moves them every evening
back down a long valley through the beauty
where Her spirit grew and Her heart is real.

Slow Dance by the Ocean

The days are hot and moist now. The doves say
true, true, true and fly lovely all the time
from and to the tree outside my window,
not quieted by the weather as the cats are.
The dogs bark only when there is a stranger.
The world moves, my Lord, and I stay still,
yielding as it passes through. I go down
the path to a bay that holds the ocean quiet,
a grassy place with oleander and broom.
When evening comes, things are clear delicately
until all is dark except the water, which is silver.
The sea takes me at night while I sleep.
During the day, memory is the pull of its huge
center. I have my dress to wash and lamps to clean
in the coming and going of time. I dance as slowly
as possible in the fields of barley and weeds.

In Dirt under Olive Trees on the Hill at Evening

Her naked body is too small for the woman's head.
The face tilts away as it listens to the music
She makes, the expression perfect happiness.
A diadem and curly hair with bits of gold
and white and red paint. The only wing left
curves from Her shoulder like the tail of a horse
prancing. Why do we care so much about the grace
of winged women, singing naked or lightly clothed?
Made by men to what purpose? A rock would do
as well, or some broken weeds. Why not the smell
of earth warmed all day by the sun, or the sense
of unseen water underground, or the sky at morning?
Why this pity, this glad humming when we see Her
sitting with tinted breasts on a little clay throne?

Women

The polar bear hasn't eaten since November
the television says. I've just turned it
on so I don't know how long that is,
but from the sound of the man's voice
it seems probably a long time. Her cubs
watch from their cave in the snow.
She looks back as she goes to find food
in case a husband has come to eat them.
Starving and guarding, she plays.
Slides a little with her thoughts
on the slope of ice. She rolls over
on her back and slides a little more.

Evening Song

I asked whatever I met and each thing that happened
if it was She: dolphins leaping at sundown,
a pine in the olive grove. I was sick with wanting,
with searching too hard. And found Her in pieces
here and there on the shore, on the mountain.
Did care, did love. But a love like those Greeks
sailing to get Helen, plowing through the sea
with engines made of wood and cloth, bodies of blood
and bones sick with their fervor. All gone, killed
by the mythic, destroyed by the grand. An importance
that abandons the human and real. The loss boundless.

Wanting to Stay

All of it moving, turning every which way,
immersing itself in air, dangling down.
Everything breathing and shelving,
leaping up at sudden notice, alive
and tingling and going with what takes it.
All of it threaded each to each, leaf to branch,
branch to trunk, to wet roots spreading down
into the earth like hands gripping hard
to keep what lives safe from danger.
I see the blur of trees joined in the twilight,
see the dark they make as I go out of their
covering to the high place and what can be seen
from there. Wanting to stay with them.
Wanting to turn back to that haven once green,
to stay with the sensuous leaves. To know
the moving, to hear the swish and murmur,
the murmuring of division and desiring.

Not Scattered Variously Far

I keep saying, "Is She here? Is that Her?"
Whatever I see. Knowing I am not far off
that way. Not far wrong. But I want more.
To see Her again. On a little clay throne
with fruit or bird. Some white on Her breasts,
pink on Her skirt. A vastness around.
I will tell Her I am here already dead.
I will bring Her my story of loss
like a broken toy and see it mended
miraculously in Her hands.
She will be smiling all the time,
gentle and glad. I will tell Her
Mother hurts me, has always saddened me.
She will tell of trouble with Her mother.
While birds sing. It will be enough.

Inside the Same as Out

There is a violent sound of too many chickens
in one place. The small sound of a child sobbing
and the mother's voice and the sobbing stops.
Someone drags a metal wagon over cobbles
in the street outside. But the sea carries
its one silence no matter what the weather makes it do.
Peace remains always where it is. Where those in love
walk for a long time and then see the other standing
by a wall. He makes a formal speech, as one plants
a tree in an empty world. As an orange is seen,
then eaten. Making a ringing anyone can hear.

A Dark Thing inside the Day

So many want to be lifted by song and dancing,
and this morning it is easy to understand.
I write in the sound of chirping birds hidden
in the almond trees, the almonds still green
and thriving in the foliage. Up the street,
a man is hammering to make a new house as doves
continue their cooing forever. Bees humming
and high above that a brilliant clear sky.
The roses are blooming and I smell the sweetness.
Everything desirable is here already in abundance.
And the sea. The dark thing is hardly visible
in the leaves, under the sheen. We sleep easily.
So I bring no sad stories to warn the heart.
All the flowers are adult this year. The good
world gives and the white doves praise all of it.

The Last Night in Mithymna

Wind heaving in the trees.
My room quiet and warm.
Me on a thin mattress
looking at the full moon.
The sky black around Her face.
The trees a different black
beneath. Content at last
with this world that matches
my life inside and out.
Heave and renewed heave
inside and out,
and the gentleness.
Lying alone in a cotton slip
at ten of the night in July
and a bare bulb hanging down
turned on. My bare feet
warm where they cross
at the ankle.
The cloth over the broken window
swells and goes flat
and swells again.

Part
Two

PART
TWO

To Be Here

The February road to the river is mud
and dirty snow, tire tracks and corncobs
uncovered by the mildness. I think I am
living alone and that I am not afraid.
Love is those birds working hard at flying
over the mountain going somewhere else.
Fidelity is always about what we have
already lived. I am happy, kicking snow.
The trees are the ones to honor. The trees
and the broken corn. And the clear sky
that looks like rain is falling through it.
Not a pretty spring, but the real thing.
The old weeds and the old vegetables.
Winter's graceful severity melting away.
I don't think the dead will speak.
I think they are happy just to be here.
If they did, I imagine them saying
birds flying, twigs, water reflecting.
There is only this. Dead weeds waiting
uncovered to the quiet soft day.

Part of Me Wanting Everything to Live

This New England kind of love reminds me
of the potted chrysanthemum my husband
gave me. I cared for it faithfully,
turning the pot a quarter turn each day
as it sat by the window. Until the blossoms
hung with broken necks on the dry stems.
Cut off the dead parts and watched
green leaves begin, new buds open.
Thinking the chrysanthemum would not die
unless I forced it to. The new flowers
were smaller and smaller, resembling
little eyes awake and alone in the dark.
I was offended by the lessening,
by the cheap renewal. By a going on
that gradually left the important behind.
But now it's different. I want the large
and near, and endings more final. If it must
be winter, let it be absolutely winter.

Considering the Moon

I love the places on your body where
the bright patina is worn down to the metal
by the touching and kissing. Toe and knee,
nose or cheek or nipple, and your belly
as you recline. Pity is where you are.
As when I heard the old man down beneath us
playing music in the snow. And the swans
flying high up past our window were like you.
How frightening it must be to be so unclothed
as you are, as it is to be empty-handed as I am.
Your body is so quiet in heaven, as though
everything that feels hunger and listens
and lives in the open is allowed to look at you.

Separation

If you came and saw me now you might remember
the two young ducks we left behind on Lesbos.
Abandoned to a Greek farmer to live at his
bare farm in the valley among fierce chickens
and without a pond. The farmer laughed
when he saw me sitting on the ground crying,
and them side by side inside the pen facing me
with their heads stretched high and bewildered,
not sure of anything any more. You would find
me skinny and my nails bitten off and my face
worn out by the months of pain. You took them
in your lap and stroked their frail backs.
You might remember how glad I was those days
high on the mountain bending down to the earth
to look at a flowering weed or something.

The Other Country

There is always singing and rejoicing.
Good people do it with their hearts and bodies.
They apprehend the sun rising in the morning.
But what of the man, was it Lorca, who saw
white flowers lying on the foreheads of the dead?
What of the snakes that wrap themselves
close around each corpse? At first above
ground, before the friends gather to call out
the names. And again underneath the earth
as it should be. Coiled three times around
to comfort each of the dead in their time
of passing, the time of leaving what they desire.
Each carried in the smooth arms of a snake
to the unknown which is finally theirs.

Esta

I think of him overturning the tables of the money
changers and the stalls of the sellers of doves.
I think of the outside of my house where most days
there are morning glories and sun on the gentians.
I go to the river by the dirt road between cornfields
under open skies to the shade and ferns and freshness
by the water. The current is powerful against me
as I swim upstream. I reach a tree that has fallen
into the river and hold on, breathing and excited
by the bright world. When I swim back to the shallows,
there are five Puerto Rican men fishing, two adults
and three boys. Hola, I say. One of the boys
says he is learning English. El rio es frio, I say.
The older man says esta, correcting me. When I get
out and start for my towel no one looks at me.
As I leave, the boy says quietly to his father,
Eso linda. I hold on to that grace as I ride
my bicycle back through the corn, the sun on me.

The Color of Many Deer Running

The air fresh, as it has been for days.
Upper sky lavender. Deer on the far hill.
The farm woman said they would be gone
when I got there as I started down the lane.
Jumped the stream. Went under great eucalyptus
where the ground was stamped bare by two bulls
who watched from the other side of their field.
The young deer were playing as the old ate
or guarded. Then all were gone, leaping.
Except one looking down from the top.
The ending made me glad. I turned toward
the red sky and ran back down to the farm,
the man, the woman, and the young calves.
Thinking that as I grow older I will lose
my color. Will turn tan and gray like the deer.
Not one deer, but when many of them run away.

Dancer Holding Still

Her husband has left and no man moves her.
A breeze might turn her face so the hair
would hang long behind her shoulders,
but no man does. She stands because her body
wants to stand. She sits for the same reason.
She sleeps on her side in the night. Years
of dark, with stars sometimes, sometimes with
summer fire in the grass. She is not waiting.
She keeps from knowing the grief of separation.
She thinks the love will not kill her. His love
is powerful in her, the way metal loves heat.

A Stranger in the Wonderful Light

This woman has no lover. She bathes and stands
after like a tree beside a river. She does not
bear children. It's late summer on the mountain
where the grass is burned pale by the heat.
She shines and nobody knows what to do with her.
Neither plowed nor reaped. Standing still.
The hooves of goats hit against stone to no
purpose, sending scree clattering over rock
in the silence and focused light. Dry scrub.
Figs on the only tree hot in the glare,
dripping syrup onto the dirt. She should speak.
The sun settles and changes, giving life
a color more glamorous than ever. She should
speak now. If she can't, she should make a sign.

Grinding the Lens

I am pulling myself together.
Don't want to go on a trip.
I have painted the living room white
and taken out most of my things.
The room has never been so empty.
Just now a banging thunder
and suddenly falling rain.
I leave the typewriter and run
outside in my nightgown and take
the cotton blanket off the line.
It is summer and I am in the middle
of my life. Alone and happy.

Love Late at Night

I leave my house at three in the morning
and follow his boot marks in the light snow,
putting my feet in his prints. I can tell
how fast he went away by the spaces between.
I hear a train as I get to the center of town.
A young man with a backpack comes toward me
on the empty street. I can tell I'm safe
because he moves all the way to the curb
to let me pass. Then a car with people comes
from the station, driving slowly on the ice.
I am looking at the distance. A worn mountain
and the sky. This time I am the mountain.
I am three-thirty in the morning. The sky is pure.
The mountain is pure in a way, being so black.
When I get near my house, I see the footsteps,
his and mine, with the prints of a cat between
where she walked sweetly while I was away.

Kept Burning and Distant

You return when you feel like it,
like rain. And like rain you are tender,
with the rain's inept tenderness.
A passion so general I could be anywhere.
You carry me out into the wet air.
You lay me down on the leaves
and the strong thing is not the sex
but waking up alone under trees after.

We Do This with Our Bodies

Taken as an animal, she yields
to that desire which devours.
Happy in yielding her body
to the other who wants this altering,
the darkness he pushes her through.
The two of them lost but alive
in the land of death on fire.
But another passion continues in her
like a great wind, like birds curving
and lapsing in the bright sky
and returning to the dreaming trees.
She tries to think in the sexual
darkness they have become, and the dark
inside that dark smelling of him.

The Conditions

You will have to stand in the clearing and see
your arms glow near ferns and roots. Hear things
moving in the branches heavy with black green.
You will be silvery, knowing death could capture
you in that condition of yielding. You will be alarmed
by everything real, even moisture. She will not
tell you there is nothing to fear. You will come
to see her and she will blaze upon you, stun you
with the radiance of a feral world. But she cannot
take you up into herself whenever you desire,
as the world can. She is the other nature,
and sexual in a way that makes the intervening flesh
thin as paper. You will feel your bones getting
lighter. You will feel more and more at risk.
You will think her shining drains you of meaning,
but it is a journey you must take. And when the sun
returns, when you walk from the forest to your world,
you will have known the land where your spirit lives.
Will have diagrams drawn by creases on your body,
and maps on your palms that were also there. Now
you will recognize them as geography. You will know
an unkempt singing you will never hear without her.

Imperfect

The gradual wearing away leaves us alive
but unintelligible. We call it aging or growing up,
ruined by love, broken and marooned by sex.
Seeing a resemblance to the three-speed Raleighs
that are the best bikes of their kind ever made,
but the factory's closed and the ones that turn up
at the Goodwill are so rusty I decide against them,
continuing to desire and grieve. Time runs out
for the objects of my longing. We are out of focus
and we are fresh. Like the eroding wonderful kore
which more and more looks like something natural.
My boyfriend asks why I am laughing (as if I had
done something unfitting) and I have to explain
that I am happy to be painting the river
and dipping my brush in it at the same time.

Singing Enough to Feel the Rain

I am alone writing as quickly as I can,
dulled by being awake at four in the morning.
Between the past and future, without a life,
writing on the line I walk between death
and youth, between having and loss.
Passion and bravery absolutes, and I don't
have anything but the memory of Aphrodite's
elbow pushing up through the dirt, golden
with the sunlight on it. I am far from there
in a hurry not to miss the joining,
struggling to explain that this worse time
is important. It is just past autumn now
and the leaves are down, wet on the road.
Some of Her shoulder showed, but not enough
to tell whether She was facing my way.
Any of it is most of it, as any part
of Cézanne is almost all of Cézanne. Now
is so late in the world that there is silence.
Heart is as beautiful as ever. What can we
expect of a woman buried in the earth?
Most of it is enough. Some of it is almost
enough. Just as I am a body too, and if he
leans down over me there will be a world.
A train goes past making an incidental sound.
Something is nourished by the loss. An ending

and beginning at once. The world does not sing,
but we do. I sing to lessen the suffering,
thinking of the factory girl Hopkins said
lived a long time on the sacrament alone.
But I also sing to inhabit this abundance.

After the Beginning

The woman is preparing her body for sleep.
She hangs the hair forward
and it almost touches her feet.
After brushing, she throws it up and back
on to her shoulders. Then splashes water
on her face twenty times.
There is someone inside her happier
than she is, waking as she goes to sleep.

A child rolls a ball to where Death stands
and waits for him to roll it back.
But Death does not touch it.
Death covers his face with his hands
and turns away. The child runs after,
wanting to play.

The woman would like a husband and child.
The desire is curled within her body.
She takes flowers into the man's house
and thinks of finding music on the radio.
He puts his cheek against her cheek,
his mouth on her naked shoulder.
There is no music. She pays attention
to his body. It is night and quiet
all around his embraces.

Nights in the Neighborhood

I carry joy as a choir sings,
but quietly as the dark
carols. To keep the wind away
so the hidden ones will come
out into the street and add
themselves to this array of
stars, constellations and moon.
I notice the ones in pain
shine more than the others.
It's so they can be found,
I think. Found and harbored.

Part
Three

The War

We were at the border and they were checking
the luggage. We had been talking about Lermontov's
novel, *A Hero of Our Time*. John liked Petorin
because he was so modern during that transition
from one history to another. I talked about Vera
and Princess Mary, the old man and the others
Petorin hurt. I said there was no reckoning for him,
that he was not held accountable as in Tolstoy
or Dostoevsky. Maybe morality does change,
I was thinking, but suffering does not. Then
a scorpion crawled from a bundle on the table.
He fell to the floor and scurried across the room.
The men were delighted. One crouched down and held
the scorpion with a ballpoint pen while he cut off
the poisoned stinger at the end of the tail,
the scorpion stretched out was as long as a hand.
The men gathered around, some with open pocketknives
held shoulder high. The man picked up the scorpion
by the tail and put it on his friend who yelped,
jumping away. The men laughed. The scorpion fell.
Another man picked it up and threw it lightly
against the wall. The scorpion fell and kept trying,
scuttling across the tiles toward the open door.
He kept his tail high, threatening, but looked tired.
Somebody else picked up the scorpion and I told John
I was going. We went outside where there was nothing.

Euridice Saved

I am filled with all things seen
for the last time. He lays with me gently
in the unfamiliar house and kisses me. When he holds
my head in his hands and arms, I dream of the real world.
I look from the mirror to the light on the floor.
I am happy with him eating bread and coffee.
This morning when I took off my shirt to bathe,
I noticed I held it in the air before me
for some time. I looked at it without perception.
When I let it fall, it did not make a noise.
Art, I was thinking, is the imitation of what
we called nothing when we lived on the earth.

The Foreign Language of the Heart

Rivas said the virgin sisters went singing across
the empty countryside, each of them dressed in white,
full of desire for the lover who had not yet come.
I see women everywhere seeking a love that changes
but never grows less. If they went away, they have
returned. Returned unchanged, but dressed in black.
If you are carrying something on your head in a bag,
one will seek you out later when you are resting.
If you are indifferent, a young woman startles you
awake early in the morning and you hear different
kinds of birds singing in the four trees. If you
still do not respond, there will be an old woman
in the hot streets wearing a dirty gray dress.
If there is nothing that can stir you, you will see
a thin, very tall Indian woman sitting every day
with her bags on the wide steps of Iglesia el Carmen
just outside the big doors accepting alms,
watching with no particular expression as you pass.

Each Thing Measured by the Same Sun

Nothing to tell. Nothing to desire.
A silence that is not unhappy.
Who will guess I am not
backing away? I am pleased
every morning because the stones
are cold, then warm in the sun.
Sometimes wet. One, two, three days
in a row. Easy to say yes and no.
Realizing this power delicately.
Remembering the cow dying on the ground,
smelling dirt, seeing a mountain
in the distance one foot away.
Making a world in the mind.
The spirit still connected to the body.
Eyes open, uncovered to the bone.

Nothing Happening

Nothing happened in the city today unless
you count the youth on a horse pushing
eleven cows across an intersection from
the field of rubble and plastic bags
to somewhere else. Or the two children
under a table set up in their doorway
with fruit on top for sale. Or me
not keeping house for any man I love
or throwing water on the hot terrace.

The Life of Literature

Very early in the morning at the edge of the capital
she is trying to get a ride. The huge machines
go past noisily, covering her with dust. She worries
about finding safe water or soda on the way.
Finally a man reaches down and helps her climb up
the wheel and over the side into the bed of the truck.
A young girl shifts to make room, then settles her
small brother's head in her lap. An old man turns
the blade of his machete away from them. When she
reaches Condega it is a quiet town. That night
she sits on a piece of cardboard in the garden
behind the house with the husband who used to live
with her. They look at the moon and talk
of poems in the book she lent him. The one
by Bashō called *The Long Road into the Deep North.*

Life on the Rio Escondido

A tire is standing in the mud
alongside the road. A horse is prancing
in the heat, gray and outsized and handsome.
A house and after a time another house
and then another. Each as poor as the next.
Each with a variation, like the naked boy
in the door of one. A boat goes slowly down
the Hidden River with soldiers on the top.
Beyond them is a larger house on a dirt bluff
with a canoe below by the swimming children.
Then green for a while and later a horse
standing by herself who neighs and turns away.
From here it is hard to see the suffering.

Inside the War

The muzak is loud, full of sighs and bongos
in the neon light, with me in a corner by the window.
I order papaya juice because it comes in bottles. A kid
is selling plastic bags of unshelled peanuts which are
threaded to a wire ring he wears on his shoulder.
A boy wants to shine shoes. A man sells little sacks
of cookies and of saltines. I buy crackers. Outside
it is getting dark. The owner tells the kid to leave.
One sells Chicklets, another cigarettes. Some people
go out and a boy pours himself water from the pitcher
on their table. The others are still, watching him drink,
then all the boys go to the far end of the restaurant.
A woman comes in and sells lottery tickets. Three men
come in with an accordion and two guitars. They walk
around in the din of muzak carrying their instruments.
I feel sorry for them, but the muzak stops and they sing
La Paloma while the boy shines shoes at a table of men
and beers and hot sauce, the white tablecloth with plastic
over it. Koo-koo-roo-koo, they sing, then sing it again.
Ya-ya-ya-yoo. Four musicians come in with three guitars
and a gourd shaker. They chat with people and watch
the trio who are singing louder and louder. I am eating
heavy chop suey made mostly of cabbage. The boy selling
Chicklets comes over, but I say no. He looks at my food
and I ask if he wants to eat. He picks up my plate,

puts it on the other side of the table and sits down.
He quickly eats the cabbage and the bread and drinks
the rest of the papaya juice. All the musicians are singing
the Mexican music, taking turns. The lights go out and oil
lamps are brought in. I walk back to my apartment through
the dying city, using my flashlight because it is
the turn of my district to have the electricity turned off.

There Is No Language in This Country

Poetry is not in Puerto Sandino. The men stop working
at noon and silently, together, with space around
each one, walk to the Comedor to eat without forks,
spoons or knives (because they were stolen once).
A few men have tablespoons in their back pocket,
the others eat with their fingers. A place where
the water must come from somewhere else to make
the fruit drinks. Or in Tamarindo where the children
who have desks carry them home on their heads
because the school has no windows or doors. They
come running to you with the cries of children who
think nothing of living in fire. All wanting their picture
taken together under the ruined tree. There is shyness
in the ones who come close, but none of this is real.
Reality is the dust color and the boy sitting alone
at the center of a bench alongside the house, one
foot on the bench in front of him, his arm wrapped
around that leg, hand cupped over his mouth,
looking at me and the scene. That is more like it.
Or the man in a hammock lying absolutely still with
his eyes open. There is a place where you can buy
beer along the road where it turns off to enter
La Paz Centro, but only those with money go there.
Cigarettes and things that people want are nowhere

else. In town, the huge doors of the church are open.
The floor is clean, but there are no people. Poetry
does not live here, unless poetry truly is
on the side of things that have no language.
Like the earth, or people who live below the line
of existence. Poetry is the voice of what has no voice
to tell the difference between sand and dirt, rocks
and heat, life and death, love and this other thing.

Part
Four

Silence Singing

It happened when we were over by the trees.
In the late evening when no one
was in the fields around.
The stillness was like a wall,
like a doorway in the wall.
Silence like the last thing known.
The one thing no one wants.
The thing everyone leaves.

I live in that silence. Everything,
every noun, is surrounded by it.
I feel the exact same happiness I felt
early, early.

I will tell him
it is possible to live here.
That poverty makes the bountiful real.
Makes the moon hold still as I have seen it.
There is no exile here in this hour,
in this kind of landscape.

If lightning ruins the fields,
if it makes a perfect fire of trees,

if the honest man is killed without
being allowed prayer beforehand,
even so it is true that stones
make the water and a joy we can hear.
We can still wade into the river and bathe.

Four-Hand Improvisation #2

I don't know what this is, she says.
It's as if I were watching a man
carrying a cage to the sea.
I don't understand why
the wooden bridge goes only a little
way out into the waves.
Truly, I don't know what this is.

(Your body is heavy with hours
in which I am not, he thinks.
There are bodies inside your body
which I cannot touch.
What parts us is time, a little table
and stars. My dying is what I have.
Yours is what you own.)

I do not know what you are.
Rain falls on the sea
and I am the water rained on.
On the beach two young goats
rear up and strike each other
with their hooves, making a sound
like darkness and then rain.
But what are you?

(Even as the last patch of afternoon
dissolves in the lawn,
you are going.
You go in the smoke, in the light,
in the road going east.
You go as boiled soup goes,
the pot singed to blackness.
You go though you do not.
Though you don't move, you go.
There you are.
Then you are gone.)

Flowers make small cries
growing out of the animal earth.
Schools of fish travel down
the coastline and the ocean
covers them over and over, endlessly.
I do not truly know you.
Just beyond the sea grasses, the hot
dunes were flawless no matter how
many times my sister and I leaped
off the top, fell sliding
on the sand and lay still.
I remember walking on hard sand
leaving no prints, the quiet calling
in the fog. Telling me I was that.
Telling me I am what I know.

(In this wilderness of light,
I am nothing.
Your being lies on my forehead
like a stone.)

———

For and Against Memory

I can think of nothing the heart finds easy,
even these two mountains I live with;
not sun and moon walking, hawks or snake:
a death I keep close to have something near me.
And your eyes like the eyes of horses running.
You turn on your side toward me and I look
at you with my whole being, powerful
because of what will be taken from me.
(A tiny sun rises above the horizon behind
this island I painted once from a ship that was
passing, the island sliding away to my right.
I painted it well because I understood exactly
how quickly I must know that foreign thing.)
I look at you with eyes of a lion, but inside
I feel the ticking. The faint counting
that begins at the beginning of being.

Strong Pomegranate Flowers and
Seeds of the Mind

You ask about the men in my past and it makes me think
of Rome falling. "After a thousand years (Saint Augustine
said) during which no foreign invader had penetrated
the walls." You and I start at the end, begin with smoke
and rubble, ruin and death. You must imagine those walls,
one and then another, as if the city were a labyrinth.
And at the center, not a bull, lion or nest of snakes,
but women and the folds of their garments which "fall
in glory" over and over after. Women who know about god
and love, about the house with colonnades looking out
one way to the sea and the other way to the ocean,
with smells of their birthplace among the trees. You must
climb over the wreckage of walls and continue on with beggars
and the wounded. Must learn about shadows and about rape,
of cleansing with water. Augustine said many attributed
the fall to a loss of faith in the pagan gods, and something
about suppression by the emperors, Gratian and Theodosius.
It is true that I have worshipped trees. I have been praying
to whatever I can get. I have found fragments of stone,
one with the breasts of a woman on it and the name Elythia
as Greek letters cut into the marble. I tell you this
because you love me and have such a serious mouth and eyes.

Four-Hand Improvisation #3

Love is in two places and I will tell you
of the one behind the other,
beyond the apple trees of unripe fruit
and green leaves. Fullness is made of pulp,
of memory compacted powerfully.
The male shifts his weight and slides,
moves his weight until he is where green
apples enter his heart. A wrong place.
Music is created the way dense seas
cast up all things time-eaten,
sea-bitten, creased with our salt.
The scent of coming and going.
We leave the way the ocean leaves.
The kind of going in which all goes,
the dense shade getting darker.
What is behind love is another love.
The rending is a reason. Not a thing alive
in nature, but nature itself.
We go down the hill into the trees
where we are stunned by a silence made
of our earthly parts. We prepare ourselves
and go toward, dragging the here.
All the evidence gone.

The Border between Things

Our meetings are like hawks mating, you said,
plunging straight for the earth, crying for
extra distance. Falling faster, the ground
very near. Simplifying in the wild rush of air.
When I was a child at Playland, we cranked
the old movies by hand. When we paused, a man
stopped. If we turned more, the man walked out
into the ordinary night of a small town
and a few cars. (I imagined cricket sounds.)
The stuttering of the scene, the constant
jerking made it somehow more real, made it
more seeable. Everything for us now is blurred
by our passion. Your shoes drop on the floor
and we immediately are together, blessed
and unreal in the rapid going forward. And yet
we search for evidence of the partial thing.
Afterwards, I stand at the window tilting
a black and white negative in the light, trying
to make it positive. Wondering if God prefers
the flickering as we cross the border from dark
to invisible. From not having to being undone.
Do we pass from loneliness to beyond without
hovering between? Leda remembered nothing
but the ecstasy. Not the gradations of tenderness

and muscle. She remembered just before, remembered
spreading her knees and the ecstasy raining down.
But not the border, not the zig-zagging back
and forth between the visible and the invisible.
Not the moment between the natural and unnatural.

These Printed Words Are a Place

These marks on paper tell of places within,
scratchings of the mind, spirit, and the other.
Records of a location where I lived for a while
and may return. Where he visits, and where
a radiance burns in him. Ordinary light
can make him vanish in the nearly empty rooms.
These words tell a story of my infinite caring,
of a quaking there as if something wants our
disembodiment. We lie naked on the mattress,
covered with the single sheet, the door closed
to make more darkness, entering another world.
The door opens by itself after, showing the light
has changed in the window of that other room
where a glass of water stands waiting on a table,
pears on a plate like gifts from centuries before.

I Wage My Life Against This Your Body

I cannot keep you with me. You must live apart,
live far off and die in order to trespass,
as the moon is filled with its own story. As music
dignifies and represents what we are and want to be.
As thistles stand with their blue translations
of the sun after the hillside poppies outside
Mithymna, windblown over the sea, have gone, have
died impossibly of their own blood-red tenderness,
and disappeared. The song, the human song of you,
is seed impregnating the cypress by the grave.
The day focuses the light for a moment just before
it ends, just before the sun goes down and evening
as always tries to make everything seem all right.

Driving to Houston

Somebody named this primitive river Vermilion.
And somebody named the town Bauxite,
as if being human was less than what
they worked at here. "I love you,
I adore you, marry me," is scrawled
on a trestle. The names are
painted out. America is big enough
for love, but too big for tenderness.

I am tired and hungry, driving at night
in humidity and fog. Once in a while
a truck parked under an overpass
with the lights on.

At three in the morning, I go through
a place where red and green traffic
lights shine against the swarthy sky
while a black man rides his bicycle
along the empty street. The houses
dark and no place open to eat.
This is the hour of my permission.
The town is called Hope.

As I cross this land, I see no feet
painted blue. No blue handprints

on the doors for safety. What man has
made is a blank thing, a created lack,
a warehouse empty of soul. *Unleaded gas,*
fried chicken. Three smashed possums so far.
A broken-down car pulling a trailer, the owner
walking around it. Nobody stopping.
Texarkana, Catfish King, "Drive through
service." *Walmart, Discount City.*
A young woman with short brown hair walking
with a sack thrown over her shoulder.
Nothingness with the trees pushed back.

We live alone in our self, close by
the suffering and say, "Did you hear
that bird? Did you see it?"
Yellow flowers under pines, a horse
completely shaded under one tree,
the shadow making it more and less
substantial.

My dearest, you are a green leaf torn
by your own hands because of love.
I could not tell you not to do it,
just as I cannot tell wind or lightning
not to damage a tree. I live inside you
as I cross the Little Cypress Bayou.
I sit on the dry wooden floor of
the damaged shack inside you, lifting
my knees to paint the bottoms of my feet
blue, my surprise for your birthday.
You did not believe I would live

---

in such a place, empty and hidden away
in the hills: old and empty, never
lived in, or lived in so long ago
it has no smell. You will come to see me
as a snake comes.

It is beguiling to realize I am wrong
in the same way year after year.
To see how exact my role is.
This time everything is clear. You will
come to the small, dry house of yourself
knowing how rare it is for anyone
to find what is absolutely theirs.
You will touch the sides of my face
with the tips of your fingers, and kiss
my upper lip without taking your mouth
away for a long time.

Driving toward Houston at six-thirty
in the evening, crossing the Trinity
River, the sky dull, the water shining
with the sun. You are in the North
at home with two children and a wife.
Here the pines grow very tall
and have no branches except at the top
where the light touches them.
The injustice of your desire recommends
its reality, now that I have moved
inside of you, to let you know
where you are.

———

It Is the Rising I Love

As long as I struggle to float above the ground
and fail, there is reason for this poetry.
On the stone back of Ludovici's throne, Venus
is rising from the water. Her face and arms
are raised, and the two women trained in the ways
of the world help her rise, covering her
nakedness with a cloth at the same time.
It is the rising I love, from no matter what element
to the one above. She from water to land,
me from earth to air as if I had a soul.
Helped by prayers and not by women, I say
(ascending in all my sexual glamour), see my body
bathed in light and air. See me rise like a flame,
like the sun, moon, stars, birds, wind. In light.
In dark. But I never achieve it. I get on my knees
this gray April to see if open crocuses have a smell.
I must live in the suffering and desire of what
rises and falls. The terrible blind grinding
of gears against our bodies and lives.

The Song

The bird is not smart. The heart
rules her as the sun does,
as the tree she lives in rules her.
Who is to say it should be different?
She does not question. She sits
on the sway of branch at evening
and knows how to distinguish
one calling from all the other
songs at the end of each day,
in the very last light.

A Flower No More than Itself

She was there on the mountain,
still as the fig tree and the failed wheat.
Only the lizards and a few goats moved.
Everything stunned by heat and silence.
I would get to the top of the terraced starkness
with my ankles cut by thistles and all of me
drained by the effort in the fierce light.
I would put the pomegranate and the anise
and a few daisies on the great rock
where the fountain was long ago.
Too tired to praise. And found each time
tenderness and abundance in the bareness.
Went back down knowing I would sleep clean.
That She would be awake all year with sun
and dirt and rain. Pride Her life.
All nature Her wealth. Sound of owls Her pillow.

Demon-Catchers on Our Doors

We walk up the valley ankle-deep in tenderness,
hunting lions without weapons. Knowing
what ripens desires to be gathered.
Ladies winnow at the threshing ring
on late summer days of singing and thirst.
It is what our strength tells us.
We gather sticks for the ritual,
the sound of animals in the air.
It takes strength to yield, to give in
to the applause of ocean and fire,
to let the bones dictate. They have been
in exile getting strength from the wildness.
We throw flowers on whatever that thing is
that roars, our hearts in our bodies.
It is right. The stars reel in the dark.
Vermeer's woman holds up the scale
to weigh the pearls in the quiet room.
And each time something happens
to make them balance in the satin light.

Printed in the USA
CPSIA information can be obtained
at www.ICGtesting.com
LVHW041102171024
794057LV00001B/202

9 781555 971731